Amazing Animals

Jinny Johnson

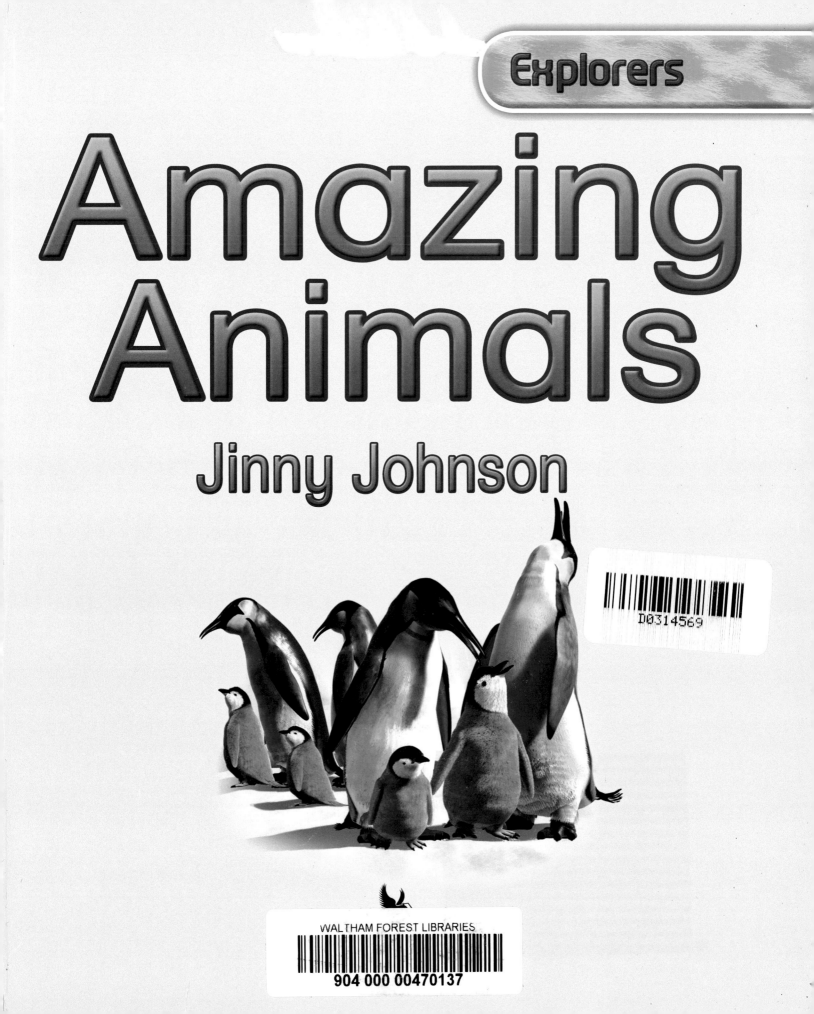

First published 2010 by Kingfisher
This edition published 2016 by Kingfisher
an imprint of Macmillan Children's Books
20 New Wharf Road, London N1 9RR
Associated companies throughout the world
www.panmacmillan.com

Illustrations by: Peter Bull Art Studio

ISBN 978-0-7534-4117-6

1 3 5 7 9 8 6 4 2
1TR/0516/UTD/WKT/128MA

A CIP catalogue record for this book is available
from the British Library.

Printed in China

Picture credits

**The Publisher would like to thank the following
for permission to reproduce their images
(t = top, b = bottom, c = centre, r = right, l = left):**

Cover: Shutterstock/Vladimir Sazonov; Pages 4cl Frank Lane Picture
Agency (FLPA)/Jurgen & Christine Sohns/
Minden; 4b FLPA/Suzi Eszterhas/
Minden; 4–5 Ardea/Rolf Kopfle; 5tl Nature Picture Library (NPL);
5tr Shutterstock/Rich Carey; 5cr NPL/David Kjaer; 6tl Shutterstock/
Justin Black; 8cl Ardea/Rolf Kopfle; 8cr Shutterstock/Kristian Bell;
8bl Ardea/Stefan Meyers; 9t Alamy/Westend61; 9cr Shutterstock/Steve
Byland; 9bl Ardea/Thomas Marent; 10bl FLPA/Nigel Cattlin;
12tr Ardea/Hans & Judy Beste; 12cl Ardea/D. Parer & E. Parer-Cook;
12br NPL/Mike Potts; 13tc NPL/Peter Oxford; 13tr FLPA/Mitsuaki
Iwago/Minden; 13b NPL/Nick Garbutt; 14tl Shutterstock/Chris Turner;
16cl Shutterstock/D...
17tl Nicky Studdart;
Jagdeep Rajput; 18
Patricia Fogden; 20
Shepherd; 21tl NPL
21b Getty/Stringer;
Steve Hopkin; 24bl
Forsyth; 25tl Shutt
25cr Naturepl/Natu
26bl Shutterstock/
28cr Shutterstock/
29cr Kelvin Aitken/
29br Corbis/Richa
30cr Shutterstock
31cl Shutterstock/

Contents

More to explore

On some of the pages in this book, you will find coloured buttons with symbols on them. There are four different colours, and each belongs to a different topic. Choose a topic, and follow its coloured buttons through the book, and you'll make some interesting discoveries of your own.

For example, on page 7 you'll find an orange button, like this, next to a tiger in the jungle. The orange buttons are about conservation.

Page 22

Conservation

There is a page number in the button. Turn to that page (page 22) to find an orange button next to another animal that needs conservation. Follow all the steps through the book, and at the end of your journey you'll find out how the steps are linked, and discover even more information about this topic.

Animal champions

Habitats

Plants

The other topics in this book are animal champions, habitats and plants. Follow the steps and see what you can discover!

A world of animals

Life for most animals is a constant struggle to survive. But animals have all kinds of amazing ways of making sure they find enough food, water and shelter. They must also care for their young and avoid hunters and other dangers.

A chameleon is a walking insect trap. It shoots out its long, sticky tongue to snatch an insect and swallows it – all in a fraction of a second.

Wildebeest move around in a herd for safety.

cheetah with young

A cheetah mum has to catch enough food to feed her hungry cubs while they are growing up. Luckily, cheetahs can run faster than any other animal, so she is a good hunter.

Lionfish use the sharp spines on their fins to protect themselves. The spines are poisonous and can give any attacker a very painful sting.

Butterflies feed on sweet, sugary nectar from flowers.

lionfish in coral reef

A lionfish has up to 18 spines that sting attackers.

Chicks gobble up insects brought by mum.

The reed warbler weaves a cosy nest from grass, leaves and spiders' webs, and lines it with wool and feathers. Here the warbler lays its eggs and looks after its young.

A young cheetah has to learn how to hunt prey.

1 Fig trees grow well in the jungle.

2 Langur monkeys love to eat figs.

3 Sambar deer are a tiger's favourite prey.

Page 14

What is this?

Jungle hunters

Lots of animals live by hunting and eating other creatures. Tigers, leopards and other big cats are some of the biggest and most successful hunters. They prey on animals such as deer. Hyenas are meat-eaters too, but they often feed on the leftovers of other hunters' meals.

A tiger slinks through the long grass towards a herd of sambar deer in an Indian jungle. Some monkeys have spotted the tiger and start shrieking loudly. The deer look up and get ready to run. A leopard is watching from a tree, but it is not as strong as the tiger so must wait its turn.

Page 23

Page 22

? This is a tiger's face. Each tiger has different markings. No two are exactly alike.

Hunters of all kinds

There are hunters in all groups of animals. Some birds, snakes, fish and insects catch other creatures to eat. Not every hunter goes after large prey. The anteater laps up huge numbers of teeny-tiny termites.

eagle ready to swoop

The bald eagle's favourite food is fish. The eagle spots its prey from the air, then swoops down to seize fish from the water in its strong claws.

The pit viper kills prey with its poisonou

pride of lions

Lions are the only big cats that live together in a group. This group is called a pride. Lions hunt together, too. The females do most of the hunting and work as a team to bring down big animals, such as buffalo.

hammerhead
shark

*The hammerhead
shark hunts fish
and squid.*

...merhead shark has a
...angely shaped head, with
...ge and one nostril at each end.
...entists think that this arrangement
...elps the shark search a wide area
of sea for prey more quickly.

A praying mantis grasps its butterfly prey.

tamandua

A tamandua's tongue
is 40cm long and has
a sticky surface, so it is
perfect for picking up ants
and termites. This anteater
flicks its tongue in and out
very fast and eats about
9,000 insects a day!

Plant-eaters

A plant-eating animal does not have to catch its food, but it does spend most of its time feeding. Plants don't fill up an animal as much as meat does, so plant-eaters have to eat large amounts to get enough energy and stay active.

ge 30

What is this?

Page 26

① Himalayan pika nibbling grass

② Himalayan tahr on the lookout

③ brown bear looking for food

? This is a close-up of an Indian moon moth's wings. The 'eye' pattern confuses predators.

Blue sheep, pikas and birds feed peacefully on grass and other plants on the lower slopes of the Himalaya mountains. A brown bear is sneaking up the hill towards them. Bears feed mainly on plant food, such as leaves, nuts and berries. But if a bear is very hungry it will attack other animals, including sheep and goats.

Page 18

6

4

5

 blue sheep feeding   Himalayan partridges   6 flowering rhododendron plants

Food from plants

Lots of plant-eaters can live together in the same area because they all want to eat different things. The animals also feed on different parts of plants. Some eat leaves and grass, but others prefer seeds, fruit and nuts.

Some bats, such as this tiny **blossom bat**, feed on nectar, a sweet liquid made by flowers, and pollen. The bat grasps the plant with its wings while it laps up the nectar with its long tongue.

marine iguana feeding on algae on rocks

A marine iguana has strong, sharp claws to help it cling to underwater rocks.

The marine iguana is the only lizard that lives in the sea. It feeds on seaweed, which it scrapes off rocks with its small, sharp teeth. When it is not feeding, this iguana comes up to the surface and sunbathes on the rocks.

A locust can eat its own weight in plants every day.

The colourful **scarlet macaw** has one of the strongest beaks of any bird. It can crack the toughest nuts and break open unripe fruit that other animals cannot tackle.

The macaw eats the flesh around the palm nut as well as the hard nut itself.

Bamboo shoots are the giant panda's main food.

A male proboscis monkey's nose can be up to 17.5cm long.

Long-nosed **proboscis monkeys** live in rainforests and feed mostly on the leaves of mangrove plants. They also eat some fruit and seeds.

Mangrove trees like this one grow along tropical coastlines. They have tough leaves and can survive being drenched with salty seawater twice a day.

1 strong teeth for cutting through wood

2 A broad tail helps the beaver steer in water.

3 The dam creates a quiet pool.

Page 18

Page 30

Page 30

What is this?

1

2

Making homes

Many animals make some kind of shelter to protect themselves and their young from the weather and from predators. The best home-builder of all is the beaver. Beaver families dam a stream to make a quiet pool, and build a lodge to live in from branches and mud.

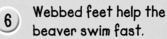

This beaver family is hard at work. On the riverbank, beavers cut logs with their strong, sharp teeth. They will add these to the dam or the lodge, or store them for winter food. The young beavers shelter inside the warm, cosy lodge.

This is a wasps' nest. Wasps make their papery nests from chewed-up wood and spit.

Amazing homes

Many birds are skilful builders. They make nests where they can keep their eggs and young safe. Other animals, including prairie dogs, badgers and rabbits, dig homes underground.

prairie dog coming out of burrow

Prairie dog families make huge underground burrows with lots of different rooms and tunnels. There are special areas in the burrow for nurseries, food stores and even toilets!

The hermit crab doesn't make its own home. It picks up someone else's. The crab's own shell is too soft to protect it, so it uses the empty shell of a snail or other creature as its home.

The weaver bird weaves an amazing nest from leaves and grass. It lays its eggs and looks after its young inside. The entrance of the nest is at the bottom, which makes it hard for hungry hunters to spot and get in.

weaver bird

red-billed hornbill at nest hole

The hummingbird makes a cup-shaped nest.

The nest is made of stems, grass and bark, held together with spiders' webs.

A female hornbill nests in a hole in a tree. Her mate helps her to seal up most of the entrance with mud so she and her young can stay safe inside. The male brings food for all the family and passes it through the hole.

hermit crab

Some wild **honey bees** make their nests in trees. The nest has just one large honeycomb and the bees cluster together on top of this.

bees' nest

What is this?

1 black-backed jackals on the prowl for prey

2 mother scorpion with young on her back

3 springbok suckling a calf

Page 10

Page 22

Family life

Meerkats are a kind of mongoose. Like most mammals, they give their babies lots of care and attention. The mothers feed their young on their own milk and keep them safe. They also teach the babies how to find food and avoid danger.

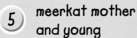

4

6

Meerkats live in groups of families. The meerkats standing up are sentries. They are watching out for danger, while others go looking for food. Young meerkats play, snack on their mum's milk and learn how to tackle a dangerous scorpion.

5

These are the meerkat's sharp claws. They help it dig underground for food and shelter.

A **poison dart frog** mother carries her newly-hatched tadpoles, one at a time, to water. She finds each one a pool of water cupped in the centre of a bromeliad plant.

tadpole on its way to its own mini-nursery pool

Ducklings follow their mother to stay safe.

An earwig mum guards her eggs and feeds her young.

Musk oxen gather in a circle round their young if a wolf or other hunter comes near. The calves are safe at the centre of the group, as few animals dare to attack full-grown musk oxen.

Caring for young

As soon as their young are born, animal parents must find ways of keeping them safe from hunters and other dangers. From earwigs to crocodiles, creatures do everything they can to protect their precious babies while they are still too young to look out for themselves.

A newly-hatched baby gets a ride in mum's toothy jaws.

gibbon mother and young

Crocodile babies hatch from eggs on land. The mother gently scoops them up and carries them to a safe area of water, where she watches over them.

Gibbons, like most apes and monkeys, take great care of their young. The mother feeds her baby on milk and it stays close to her for several years.

musk oxen and young in the Arctic

Danger in the savannah

Many different plant-eaters live on the African grasslands called the savannah. There is plenty of food, but all these animals must be on the alert for danger. They each have their own way of defending themselves.

Page 10

Page 14

What is this?

1 pangolin with its armour of heavy scales

2 Elephants are protected by their size.

3 gazelle being chased by a cheetah

? These are a zebra's stripes. They confuse predators so they don't know where to attack.

Gazelle scatter in alarm as a fast-running cheetah closes in. Gazelle are speedy, too, so if they spot the cheetah in time they can escape. Like many grassland grazers, gazelle stick together in herds. There is safety in numbers. Nearby, some elephants stay close to a young calf. A full-grown elephant is just too big for most hunters to tackle.

5

6

Page 27

4 Tall giraffes can spot danger from afar.

 5 vervet monkeys high in the trees

 6 zebras sticking together in a group

Attack and defence

Animals have some amazing weapons for defending themselves and attacking prey. They bite, sting and poison their enemies. The bombardier beetle even creates an explosion and sprays boiling liquid from its body.

charging
black rhino

Black rhinos are usually peaceful animals but will attack if they are disturbed. A charging rhino can run faster than a person and is a terrifying sight. Its huge front horn can be over 50cm long.

The wandering spider has a poisonous bite.

spines up to
30cm long ·······

umbrella-shaped body
with tentacles
trailing below ·······

porcupine

Jellyfish look pretty
but can give a nasty sting.
All over the tentacles are
tiny little stinging cells.
These contain poison
and can be shot out
at an enemy.

A bombardier beetle sprays out boiling-hot liquid.

Most of the time, a **porcupine**'s
spines rest flat against its body.
But when alarmed, its spines stick
up and rattle. The noise warns the
enemy to go away. If it doesn't,
the porcupine runs at it, ramming
its spines into the enemy's skin.

skunk squirting
in self-defence

smelly liquid
jets out here

The skunk is
well known for
being smelly! When in
danger it sprays a nasty
liquid. The liquid irritates its
attacker and may even blind
it for a while. This gives the
skunk a chance to escape.

Survival!

Animals manage to survive in even the coldest places on Earth. Seals and penguins stay warm thanks to extra layers of body fat and thick fur or feathers. Some birds just fly in for the summer, when the weather isn't as cold.

Page 30

What is this?

1 Skuas steal penguin eggs and chicks.

2 Rival male elephant seals do battle.

3 Leopard seals chase fish and penguin chicks.

? This is an orca's fin. An orca is a kind of dolphin that hunts fish, seals and penguins.

Emperor penguins huddle on the ice, watching their chicks dive into the freezing water for the first time. Two elephant seals battle with each other on an ice floe, while speedy leopard seals hunt fish.

6

4 Snow petrels stay here in Antarctica all year round.

5 Penguin chicks take their first swim.

 6 emperor penguins, the largest of all penguins

Some honeypot ants eat so much they swell up like living storage jars. When food is scarce, they 'throw up' to feed the other ants. Yuck!

honeypot ants in the desert

The fennec fox is the smallest of all the foxes, but it has very big ears. Its over-sized ears help it lose heat from its body in its hot desert home.

Most crocodiles live in fresh water, but the saltwater crocodile can survive in the sea. It has special glands that help get rid of salt from its body.

saltwater crocodile, the largest of the crocodile family

Guanacos live high in the Andes mountains.

Staying alive

It can be very hard to live near the poles, in the desert, on high mountains or in the deep sea, but there are a surprising number of animals in all these places. They have found ways of managing to survive in their difficult homes and coping with the extreme conditions.

ears are up to 15cm long

fennec fox

The prickly football fish lives in the deep sea.

Lure shines to attract prey.

This desert beetle has a clever way of collecting water. In foggy weather, it lowers its head so moisture trickles down its back into its mouth.

fog-basking beetle

polar bear with cubs

Female polar bears give birth in the winter in a cosy den under the snow. They stay in the den until spring, when the cubs come out for the first time.

Animal champions

Hyenas have record-breaking jaws. They can crunch up bones, teeth and even hooves.

striped hyena

The sleek **cheetah** can outrun any other land animal over short distances. It can race along at 110km/h – faster than an Olympic sprinter.

Plants

rhododendron

Beautiful **plants** grow on the slopes of the Himalayas. Many are now popular garden plants.

The dry desert is a tough place for plants. To reduce water loss, the **welwitschia** has just two, very long, curling leaves. Some desert plants – cacti – have sharp spines instead of normal leaves.

Habitats

Jungles or rainforests are home to more kinds of animal and plant than anywhere else on Earth. Some Indian jungles are wet all year round; others have a dry winter season.

In northern areas with long, cold winters, very different forests grow. **Coniferous forests** have evergreen trees with narrow, needle-like leaves.

conifers

Conservation

In the last 100 years the number of **tigers** in the wild has dropped from more than 100,000 to less than 4,000. For tigers to survive they need large reserves where they can live in safety.

Forty years ago hundreds of **elephants** were killed every week for their tusks. Now selling ivory is banned, but some people still want to buy it, so the killing goes on.

More to explore

The **Arctic tern** makes one of the longest journeys of any bird. Every autumn it flies south to Antarctica and every spring it flies north again – a round trip of up to 40,000km.

Arctic tern

Beavers are champion builders. The dams they make can change the look of an area and be more than 3m high. One beaver dam in Canada was 850m long.

African savannah

Some rain falls in grassland areas. **Grass** grows from near its base as well as from its tip. That means it can carry on growing even after grazing animals have cropped it down.

Redwood trees grow where there is plenty of rain and they are among the world's most amazing plants. They can tower 100m tall or more and can live for over 1,000 years.

Deserts are the driest places on Earth and have less than 10cm of rain a year. Most are hot. Global warming and overgrazing are turning more land to desert so some deserts are becoming larger.

Namib desert

Many **alpine (mountain) animals** get the best of two habitats. They spend summer high up, feeding on fresh new grass. In winter they return to the lower slopes to avoid the worst of the weather.

Himalayan tahr

The beautiful **tragopan** used to be shot for food. Now this bird is protected by law but it is still in danger. Some areas of its forest home have been cut down.

The **Antarctic** is changing because of global warming. But polar creatures are used to the cold – higher temperatures are likely to upset the delicate balance of life there.

Index